Dedicated to my family, friends, neighbors, and students

-Mrs. Dorcely

This book belongs to:

Joumou is the Haitian Creole word for pumpkin.

During slavery, the Haitians slaves made soup Joumou, but only the slave masters were allowed to drink the soup.

On January 1, 1804,
Haiti's independence was declared.

Grandma says, "As a symbol of freedom, the Haitians made and drank soup joumou to celebrate." Now, I enjoy helping my grandma cooking soup Joumou on January first.

Time to make soup joumou!

Grandma says, "Let's get the ingredients."

We need:

joumou
meat
cabbage
celery
scallion
watercress
sweet potato
dumplin
g

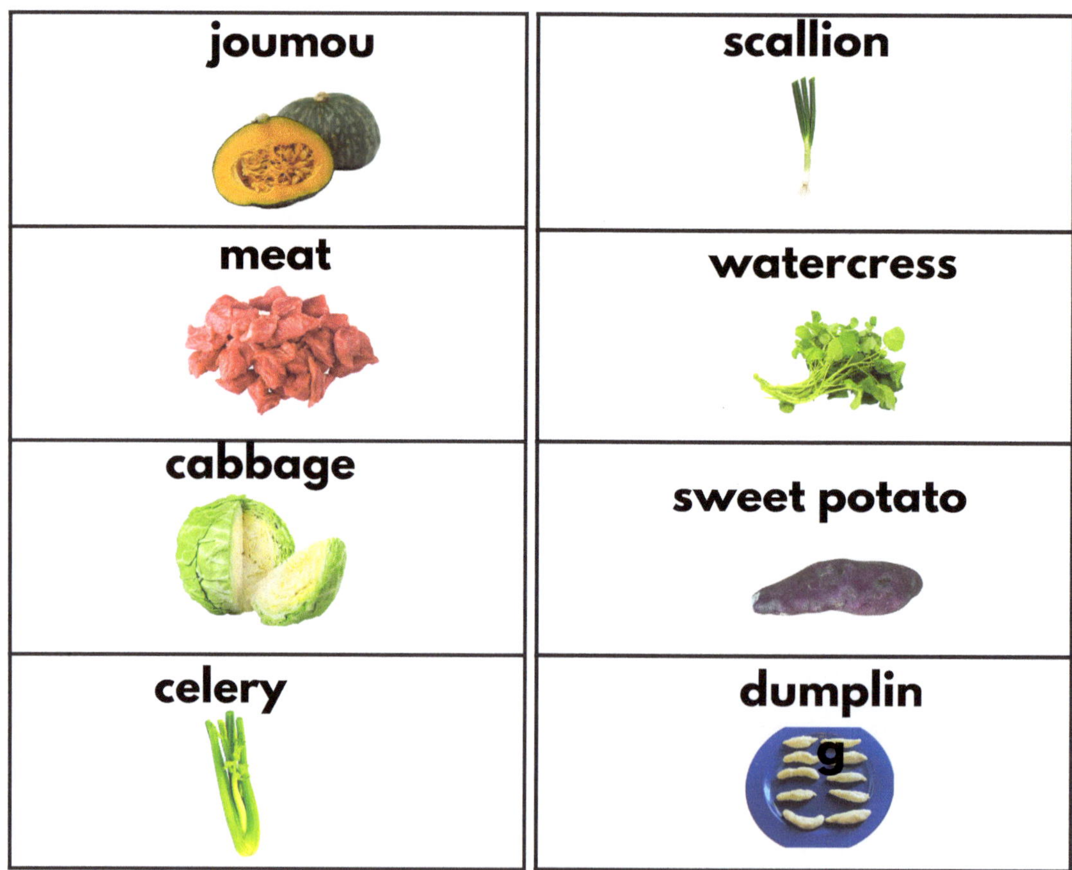

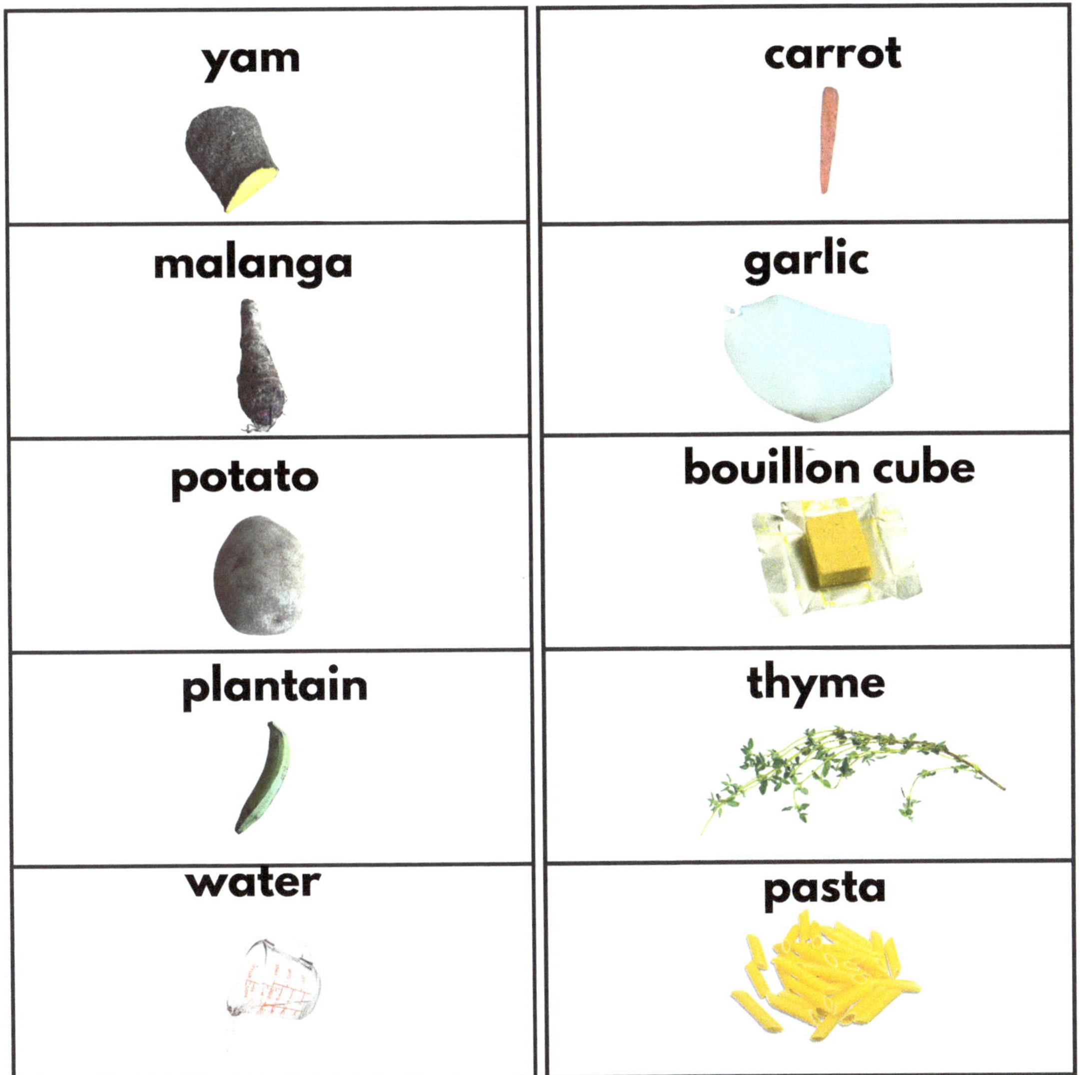
yam
carrot
malanga
garlic
potato
bouillon cube
plantain
thyme
water
pasta

We peel the yam.

We peel the malanga.

We peel the potato.

We peel the plantain.

We peel the sweet potato.

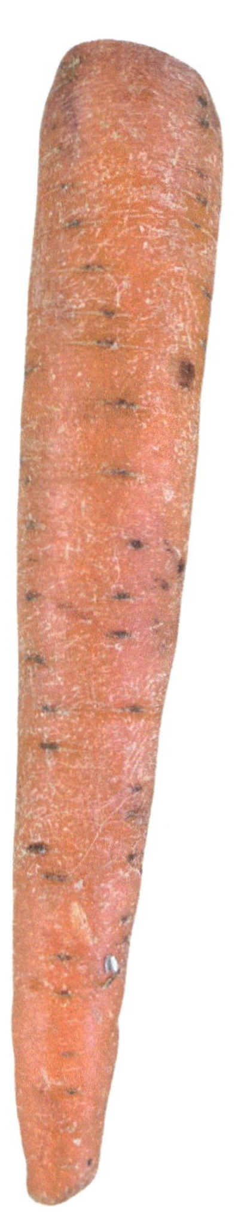

We peel the carrot.

We wash the vegetables.

We cut the vegetables.

We precook the meat.

We chop the green cabbage.

We put the chopped green cabbage in the pot.

We cut the celery.

We put the celery in the pot.

We cut the scallion.

We put the scallion in the pot.

We put the thyme in the pot.

We put the carrots in the pot.

We put the malanga in the pot.

We put the yam in the pot.

We put the potato in the pot.

We put the plantains in the pot.

We put the sweet potato in the pot.

We wash and chop the watercress.

We put the watercress in the pot.

We peel and grate the garlic.

We put the grated garlic in the pot.

We put six pieces of joumou in the pot.

Next, we are going to make dumplings.

We need:

bowl

spoon

1/2 cup of flour

1/4 cup of water

1/8 teaspoon of salt

1/2 teaspoon of butter

Pour water

Add salt

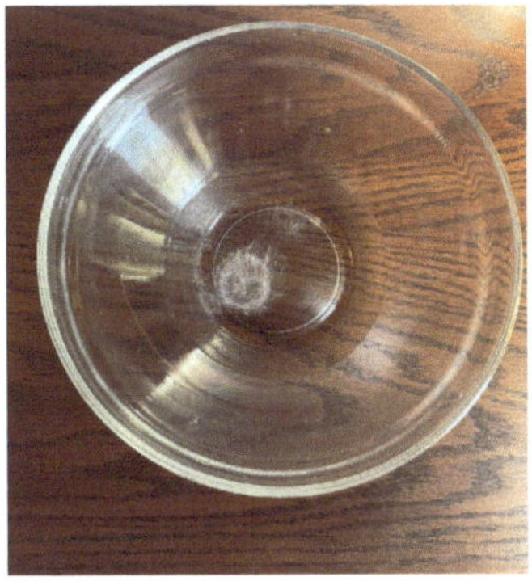

Add flour

Add butter

Mix

Make the dumplings

We make the dumplings.

We put ten dumplings in the pot.

We pour six cups of water in the pot.

We put one bouillon cube in the pot.

We let all the ingredients boil and cook.

The ingredients are cooked.

We take the joumou out of the pot to cool off.

We put the pasta in the pot.

We mash the joumou.

We add one cup of water to mashed joumou.

We pour the joumou puree in the pot.

We let the soup joumou boil.

The delicious soup joumou is ready to eat!

As a tradition, Haitians share the soup joumou with family, friends, and neighbors to celebrate independence day and the New Year.

Your turn! What is a dish from your country that means something to you?

Draw or cut a picture of a dish from your country you want to talk about.

Draw a picture of a dish from your country and write about it.

List the ingredients you need.

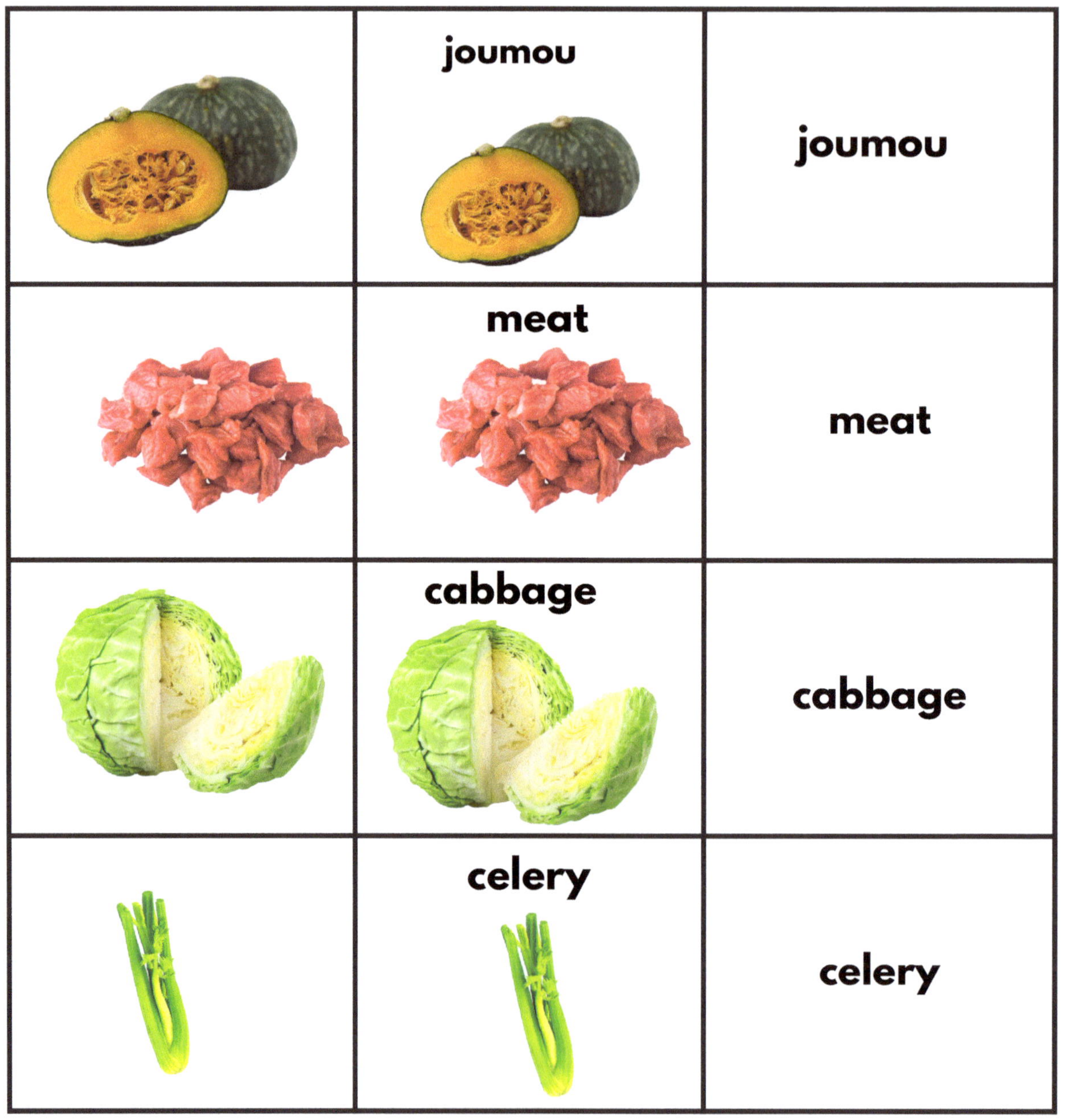
joumou
joumou
meat
meat
cabbage
cabbage
celery
celery

	scallion 	scallion
	watercress 	watercress
	sweet potato 	sweet potato
	dumpling 	dumpling

yam
yam
malanga
malanga
potato
potato
plantain
plantain

	carrot 	carrot
	garlic	garlic
	bouillon cube 	bouillon cube
	thyme 	thyme

	water 	water
	pasta 	pasta
	precooked meat 	precooked meat
	soup joumou 	soup joumou

www.ingramcontent.com/pod-product-compliance
Lightning Source LLC
LaVergne TN
LVHW070147110826
845147LV00002B/344
9798986863160